Her Own Demons

A Shocking True Crime Story

Rod Kackley

Published by Rod Kackley, 2019.

HER OWN DEMONS

First edition. May 4, 2019.

Written by Rod Kackley.

"Something happened in her brain that made her snap. She had her own demons."

----Bradon Riess

One

DAVID RIESS IS CONFRONTED with a gun in his face, inside his rural Blooming Prairie, Minnesota home. The person holding the handgun, has never killed before. But after blowing through a half-million-dollar inheritance at the casino gambling tables in Iowa; this is a person who feels like there's nothing left to lose. But if this lover of high-stakes poker tables and slot machines can get just a few thousand more dollars, maybe lady luck will smile again.

David is the one with something to lose — his life —and he does. David is shot twice with a 22-caliber semi-automatic handgun. The killer doesn't show any mercy, but, for some reason, can't just let the corpse lie where it fell. The murderer puts the gun away and lays out David's body on the floor of the bathroom. The killer then covers the corpse with towels and then rolls up another before wedging it between the bathroom door and the floor.

Serious crime is a stranger to most of those who live in the southern Minnesota community of Blooming Prairie. For instance, a City-data.com study showed there was precisely one registered sex offender living in Blooming Prairie as of March 26, 2019.

To say Blooming Prairie is rural is not a stretch. Every single one of the 1,976 people who call it home lives in what city people could describe as "the country." Maybe this is one of those upscale community that draws the rich to a secluded pastoral gated community? Hardly. The estimated median household income in 2016 was $55,646. That's about $10,000 less than the Minnesota state average.

The average house in Blooming Prairie is worth about $123,320 compared to the average worth Minnesota-wide of $211,800.

Not only is it decidedly middle-class and rural, but Blooming Prairie is one small town. There are only two churches — First Lutheran Church and St. Columbanus Church.

Blooming Prairie children begin their scholastic careers inside Blooming Prairie Elementary and then move on to Blooming Prairie High School. Since there is only one of each, there's no need to give either school a name beyond "Elementary School" and "High School."

The city's website notes that the school buildings replaced structures now known as the "Old Elementary School," and, you guessed it, the "Old High School."

The Blooming Prairie Branch Library is open every day of the week, except Tuesday and Sunday.

There are five city parks including, Central Park and eighteen businesses listed on the city's website, not including the company owned by the late David Riess and a partner; the Prairie Wax Worm Farm.

Blooming Prairie might not seem like much at first glance. But take another look at the community during the Fourth of July. You'll see one of the largest celebrations of that summer holiday in the Midwest as 35,000 people "flock to our city to celebrate our country's independence," brags the city's website. "Ask anyone, and they will tell you that this is the place to be."

As did many Midwest and prairie-state communities in the nineteenth century, Blooming Prairie began as a railroad town. It was populated mostly by the men and their families working for Minnesota Central Railroad. Of course outside of town, farmers built homes, barns, and found the land perfect for growing wheat. That sparked the construction of a flour mill.

When they arrived, and before the wheat was planted, settlers found a land covered by tall grass as far as any eye could ever see, which led the wife of one of the first settlers, to call it a "blooming prairie." It isn't known if the word "blooming" was used as a sign of disgust or was just a remark prompted by all of the growing grass.

But whatever the motivation, the name stuck.

So, except for that immense Independence Day celebration, which grows the town's population by a multiple of thirty-five, there's nothing truly exceptional about Blooming Prairie.

At least there wasn't until someone pulled the trigger on that handgun twice and took David Riess' life.

Now the people who make their homes in this small, farming community have to deal with the death of one of their own. It's a homicide that will capture the imagination of the Midwest and even the national mainstream press because the killing of David Riess and the pursuit of his murderer is just the beginning of a shocking true crime story.

Two

Blooming Prairie Police receive a call from David's business partner who says no one has seen David at their business, Prairie Wax Worm Farm, for more than two weeks.

It's time for what police everywhere call, "a welfare check." No emergency. Just a nice quiet visit, they hope. And, why would they believe otherwise. After all, this is Blooming Prairie.

Officers pull up in front of Riess' home and get inside at 7:38 pm CST. Immediately they are confronted with the worst-case scenario no cop wants. They find the fifty-four-year-old man dead inside the home, laying on the bathroom floor.

The killer probably left him lying where he died. Moving David's body out of the bathroom wouldn't have been easy. He's not a small man.

Heavy-set with thick almost curly hair, David's a big guy who looks years younger than his age. He's got "Minnesota" written all over him.

And, why not? David was born and raised in Rochester, Minnesota and went to Mayo High School. After getting his diploma, David enlisted in the U.S. Navy, serving from 1982 to 1985. He was stationed in California, married in San Diego in 1982, and served in Guam before moving back to Rochester.

Back in Minnesota, David gets a job at Crenlo. Now, this is a company with a Minnesota flavor, too. Started in the early 1950s by three guys with an entrepreneurial dream, Crenlo manufactures semi-truck cabs and cabinets for office and home. Kind of like the three partners who started Crenlo, David harbors a hope of striking out on his own, starting his own business.

He loves, is even passionate, about hunting, fishing, and boating. So, what business could he be better suited for than opening a small bait shop in Rochester?

Along with a partner, David ran the bait shop for several years. It was successful, but the pair decided to sell the store. As the sport and recreational fishing industry was taking off, David and his partner open the Prairie Wax Worm Farm in 2005, growing the bait for their fellow sports fishermen and running the business out of the Riess home on U.S. Highway 218 just southeast of Blooming Prairie.

Along with running the business, David spends a lot of time outdoors with his five grandchildren.

However, as David's obituary in the *Post Bulletin* would read with incredible understatement April 9,2018, "he passed away unexpectedly."

After discovering David's body, Blooming Prairie Police immediately call the Dodge County Sheriff's Office and turn the case over to that department. After all, the cops in Blooming Prairie see as little serious crime as do the people they are sworn to protect and serve.

So, this night and the following two days, the people of this small rural community are treated to a display of Dodge County Sheriff's Office squad cars blocking the entrance to the Riess home while the Minnesota Bureau of Criminal Apprehension does a crime scene investigation of the house.

Obviously, this is highly unusual in Blooming Prairie. The town's on alert. Everyone knows something happened, little bits of information dribble out. But other than those scraps and the usual gossip and innuendo, Blooming Prairie is in the dark. Sheriff Scott Rose refuses to release any substantial information. People in town are talking about a murder, but no one wearing a badge will confirm that story.

However, Blooming Prairie Police Chief Greg Skillestad tells reporters late Saturday afternoon there's no reason for people in town to be worried.

At 2:30 Sunday morning, Sheriff Rose comes close to telling Blooming Prairie what his people are working on. He says, "This is a very active ongoing investigation, and when we are able to, we will release more information regarding this incident and those involved. Until then, we have no additional information available."

That doesn't ease anyone's fears in Blooming Prairie. Everyone knows that if there weren't a big story brewing in the Riess' home, Sheriff Rose wouldn't have a problem telling them what was going on.

Sunday night, the Minnesota Bureau of Criminal Apprehension finally makes the announcement that confirms at least some of the public speculation.

BCA officials say they are indeed conducting a "suspicious death investigation" after the discovery of a "male subject that was found deceased." Everybody knows that has to be David. What the BCA statement says next sends an emotional shockwave through Blooming Prairie.

Everyone in town knows that no one has heard from Lois Riess. This is a small town. Why wouldn't she be talking to neighbors? Why hadn't anyone seen her around town? Lois is hard to miss. Standing 5-foot-5, and weighing 165 pounds, Lois is a happy, almost boisterous soul, an extrovert with brown eyes and platinum-blond, almost white, shoulder-length hair.

Where is Lois?

She certainly couldn't be camping out at home while the police were inside tearing everything apart.

In fact, Lois was not home during the investigation, and she wasn't there when police arrived.

So, Dodge County deputies and BCA officials want to find her, too. They say Lois is a "person of interest" in the investigation. She's not a suspect, the BCA stressed, but a "person of interest" who "may have information regarding this investigation."

And everyone in Blooming Prairie knows the BCA is serious. State investigators also issue a statewide crime alert along with a photo of the car they think Lois might be driving.

Later Sunday, Sheriff Rose tells Blooming Prairie that the dead man inside the Riess' home was in fact, David. And even though Lois is still not identified as a suspect, Rose says she might be carrying a gun and anyone who sees her should call 911 instead of taking the law into their own hands.

The sheriff also mentions that he's heard Lois likes casinos. And she has, Sheriff Rose comes to find out, a history of losing at the gaming tables and slot machines

Three

Along with telling everyone who lives in Blooming Prairie and every cop in Minnesota that Lois Riess is now something more than just a person of interest, driving a white, 2005 Cadillac Escalade with Minnesota plates, 864 LAE; Sheriff Rose and his team discover today Lois has been taking money out of David's business account.

BCA investigators find out Lois transferred $10,000 from Prairie Wax Worm Farm's account to her personal bank account. Then, she moved $11,000 from David's bank account to hers. Detectives also discover Lois has been forging David's signature on bank checks.

Lois also owes more than $100,000 to her older sister, Kimberly Sanchez. Lois took the money from her sister when she was acting as a guardian and conservator for Kimberly, who's been classified as a "vulnerable adult."

Attorneys representing Kimberly tried in 2015 to have Lois removed as Kimberly's guardian after investigators discovered she'd taken tens of thousands of dollars from her sister's account. Much of that money, the attorneys say, was gambled away by Lois at casinos.

Now, she's definitely more than just a "person of interest," no matter what Sheriff Rose might be saying to the public.

It doesn't take much of a law enforcement leap of faith to figure out that Lois, who is known to love casinos and gambling, might be moving money around to feed her habit.

Now, think about it. Where might she be?

How about her favorite casino?

Sure enough. While the cops are battering down the door of Lois' house and tramping over every inch of the Riess family home, Lois is on her way to the Diamond Jo Casino across the Minnesota state line in Iowa.

The weather could be worse. It's Minnesota, after all. Outside it's cloudy and windy with temps in the forties. Typical for March. Lois doesn't mind it much, but she's going to feel much warmer and much safer, as soon as she gets settled for the day in her second home, the Diamond Jo Casino.

Just off I-35, Diamond Jo boasts 925 slots 23 table games and a no-limit poker room, inside its faux log cabin buildings, along with bands on the weekends in the casino complex's Big Wheel Bar.

On top of that, there are four restaurants in the complex, a meeting room and event center, and a Country Inn & Suites hotel, which is attached to the casino building.

Inside today, wearing a long, button-up-the-front grey and white sweater, while her husband's body is on its way to a cold metal autopsy table, is Lois Riess.

The jovial fifty-six-year-old grandmother stopped for fuel and a sandwich outside the casino at the Kum and Go gas station before settling down on one of the red bar stools in front of one of the hundreds of Diamond Jo slot machines.

Of course, big money is wagered in the no-limit poker room and at the table games. There's plenty to keep Lois occupied for the day. She has to be a sitting duck for the Dodge County Sheriff's Office and the BCA.

But, no. Lois doesn't sit long, at least not long enough.

Investigators know where to find her. And that's where they go, to the Diamond Jo Casino. Unfortunately, Lois, intentionally or not, is a step ahead of the law. After spending most of Sunday playing the games, Lois leaves the casino just before Dodge County Sheriff's Office squad cars pull into the parking lot.

Not long after that, a friend of Lois' in Blooming Prairie gets a phone call from a woman named "Stormy Liberty" who asks for the address of a woman she says is a mutual friend, Theresa Koster.

Theresa has a winter home in Fort Myers, Florida, Stormy says to Theresa. She wants to visit and just needs the address. Although the woman who received the call is suspicious, she gives Theresa's information to Stormy and hangs up wondering who she just talked to.

Stormy is actually Lois. She has a cellphone account in the name of "Stormy Liberty" and is now using that phone and that alias.

Thanks to her friend in Blooming Prairie, Lois isn't planning on spending a moment longer in Minnesota than necessary.

Lois, being actively sought by police and state officials as a "person of interest" in her husband's death, has no interest in David's murder, if she's even aware of the crime.

And, forget the cloudy, forty-degree weather of Minnesota. Lois is on her way to Theresa's house in Fort Myers.

Four

APRIL 4, 2018

Lois leaves the so-called "early Spring" of Minnesota behind as she drives as quickly south as possible. By the time she travels down I-35 through Iowa and then Missouri, and pushes into early April, her memory of Blooming Prairie temps in the 40s fades under the pastel skies and sunshine of Fort Myers.

At eight a.m. this day, the dashboard of the Cadillac Escalade shows it is already 82 degrees outside.

Lois isn't alone in enjoying the morning's warm, humid weather. Theresa "Tess" Koster's feeling good, too. It is a beautiful day in Fort Myers. But she is more accustomed to the wonders of April in Florida than is Lois. After all, Theresa's had her winter home in Fort Myers for some time. It sure beats Minnesota.

So, like most days, Theresa goes outside to enjoy the morning air—afternoons even in April can be a bit oppressive, the best time to be outdoors is before noon—and she sees a woman staring at her car. What the heck? This isn't right, Theresa thinks. The woman's middle-aged, maybe in her fifties, rather large, at least she hasn't missed too many meals; and the crazy thing is, Theresa recognizes her. Or at least she thinks she does. Her brain sorts through the image sent by her eyes and realizes it could only be one person. Is that Lois Riess? What's she doing down here? Doesn't she know David's dead? Murdered?

Lois is no stranger. She and Dave were guests of Theresa and Rodney Koster at their winter home several months ago. They'd had drinks and dinner together. So, why she standing over there like a lurking stranger?

Today, this morning, their eyes meet. Theresa opens her mouth to say, "Hello?" in a questioning manner. But, before she can say a word, Lois waves, says, "wrong house, wrong house," gets into her Escalade, and drives away, quickly, leaving Theresa standing in her driveway wondering what the hell just happened.

It would all seem so odd if Theresa hadn't been watching CNN. The story of David Riess' murder in Minnesota and his missing wife, Lois, has made the national news. No one with a cable subscription could miss it.

Of course, Theresa pays rapt attention to the story every time it recycles on cable news. Who can blame her since she actually knows the people involved? How many times does that happen?

It wasn't just CNN. Fox News, MSNBC, every cable station had it. Even if Theresa didn't count David and Lois as friends, she'd feel like she knew them now, if only because their pictures were on her flat screen every thirty minutes.

Lois, for lack of a better expression, Theresa realizes, is a wanted woman. The cops in Minnesota are still referring to her as a "person of interest." Theresa has no doubt authorities want to find Lois and talk to her. So she does what most good citizens born and raised in the Midwest would do. She hurries inside and calls Fort Myers police.

And breathlessly Theresa tells them, she's just seen, Lois Riess.

Lois knows she's made a mistake. God, what was she thinking? The instant she locks eyes with Theresa, Lois knows that she has blown it. Was she thinking of stealing Theresa's car? Maybe. Lois knows the police had to have a description of her Cadillac and its license plate. She needs a new ride. A new name would help too. The alias, "Stormy Liberty" is only going to take her so far. Lois needs a new name, a new identity, a fresh start in life. That means credit cards.

So much to do. There's no time to beat herself up over what happened at Theresa's house.

She is driving quickly. Not too fast though. There is no need to attract attention. Even if Theresa calls the police, Lois is still only driving one Cadillac of the thousands piloted by white-and-blue hairs in Fort Myers. This is Florida after all.

So there is no reason to panic. There's only one mission: building a new life.

However, besides the pressure of her paranoia and stress, Lois is tired and hungry. Twenty-four hours and nearly 1,600 miles on the road aren't easy. It had been a long drive from Diamond Jo's. She needs a break.

Lois isn't a stranger to Fort Myers. As Theresa remembered, she and Dave had been down here before.

Lois pulls into the Smoking Oyster Brewery's parking lot, one of their favorite places, for a rest. She'll feel better inside. Food and a drink, or two, will help.

Sliding on to a bar stool, Lois is relaxing a bit, coming down from all the time on the road, when she stops and stares at another woman. Why does this woman look so damn familiar?

This isn't someone she knows. This woman isn't one of the snowbirds from Blooming Prairie who spends winters in Florida. She is a stranger, but at the same time, Lois feels like she is looking in a mirror.

"Whoever this woman is, she looks just like me," Lois says to herself. Same eyes, same size, same almost-white hair.

Lois stares a moment while she feels the stress and pressure fading away. Those emotions are replaced by something new: hope.

With only a slight hesitation, Lois walks up to her mirror image and says, "Hello."

Five

Considering they've only known each other for a day-and-a-half, Lois and her new friend, Pamela Hutchinson, couldn't be closer. It's not just that they feel like they've known each other all of their lives; these two women look enough alike to be sisters.

And maybe they are, as much time as they're spending together.

The two new BFF's spent most of yesterday and last night together. Lois and Pamela had drinks and dinner together at the Smoking Oyster Brewery. It was a great night, chatting, eating, and drinking. They really got to know each other and find out how much they had in common.

Smoking Oyster Brewery bills itself as the "classiest dive and Fort Myers Beach." The locals just call it "S.O.B." and along with its casual island atmosphere, burgers, seafood, beer, and drinks; it sells fun. And Lois and Pam are having plenty of all Smoking Oyster has to offer.

The two women who have become fast friends aren't the only ones in the restaurant who've noticed how much they look alike.

Being each other's "doppelgänger" has become a topic of conversation among those serving them, too.

Pamela feels like Lois is just what she needs. Brand new to Fort Myers Beach—she just moved here a year ago from her hometown of Virginia Beach, Virginia—Pamela feels fortunate to have met someone so open and friendly, and so much in the know about the area.

Up early this morning, Pamela has already called the front desk of the hotel-condo where she's staying—Lois has moved in, too—to extend the reservation on her suite for another three days. Why bring such a good time to an early and abrupt ending? It's easy enough to do. Pamela gives the desk clerk her credit card number, it goes through as smoothly as she knew it would and bingo, three more days of fun with her new buddy, Lois.

Later in the day, Pamela withdrew $5,000 from her Wells Fargo bank account. And now, for some reason, she's on her way to Ocala, Florida. The town of about 59,000 people is three hours north of Fort Myers and some forty or fifty miles inland from the Gulf Coast.

Ocala doesn't have the party atmosphere of Fort Myers or Fort Myers Beach where she and Lois have been having so much fun, but it's got a lot going for it. Silver Springs State Park's Silver River with its kayaks and glass-bottom boats shouldn't be missed by anyone touring Florida.

And it's a nice hotel, Pamela's booked herself into. As lovely as the hotel-condo in Fort Myers Beach? Maybe not. But still nice. There's a vacancy, too.

She doesn't have a reservation, but it's simple enough to get a room. Pamela just drives up to the front door, goes inside, shows her credit card, and she's in.

Once in her room, Pamela makes herself comfortable for the night. She orders room service, a movie and puts it all on her credit card.

The only thing—or person—missing is Lois. She's nowhere to be seen. Must have decided to stay on the Gulf Coast in Fort Myers Beach. Maybe she'll go back to see Tess Koster, and they'll have a real visit.

Six

Pamela Hutchinson isn't in Ocala, this morning. In fact, it appears, she never was. Lee County Sheriffs deputies and detectives, however, know where she is at this exact moment. They have incontrovertible proof.

Pamela's in the bathroom of room 404 of the Marina Villa hotel/condo at Snug Harbor in Fort Myers Beach. Talk about being indisposed. She's laid out on the floor, resting on a pillow with a towel draped over her face and torso. She's dead. Shot twice with a small-caliber semi-automatic handgun, once in the heart and once in her side. Looks like she was shot in the bedroom, the master bedroom, and dragged into the bathroom.

Pamela posted a message on her Facebook page four days ago, April 5, about watching the sunrise and hearing music from the Smoking Oyster. Then Pamela wrote that she'd decided to stay an extra day.

That was the last anyone who knew Pamela heard from her. Friends and relatives had become concerned.

They were right to worry. But it is too late.

A hotel maid opens the door after knocking and getting no response. This is the day Pamela is supposed to be checking out, and the hotel needs to get the suite ready for the next paying guest. So the maid has to go in. She finds Pamela's dead body.

Troy Strohm, who is staying in the room a floor below Pamela, hears the maid yelling. He runs upstairs and into what turned out to be Pamela's next-to-final resting place.

As soon as he opens the door, Troy knows what had happened, or at least what he would find.

Rather than the fresh smell of an upscale hotel room, his nostrils are assaulted by the rotting stink of a dead animal

Troy, the maid, and the detectives who followed, not only find Pamela's dead body. They discover the room is a real mess. Someone, probably the killer, had ransacked it, going through her purse too. There isn't a single credit card in the bag, including the one she'd use to extend her stay. And there is no money in the purse either, so police are figuring the killer got the cash too.

Outside in the parking lot, there is no sign of the white Accura TL with Florida plates that Pamela was driving when she arrived at the hotel.

Lee County detectives take a look at hotel security video tape, along with tape from the S.O.B. a few nights before. Guess who they see on the tapes. And guess who is nowhere to be found, even though hotel employees say that she's been staying with Pamela for the past couple of days.

The Lee County Sheriff's Office has seen the bulletins from Blooming Prairie. Now, they know they're looking for the same woman, Lois Riess. And they're pretty confident Lois killed Pamela. Lee County detectives think they know why she pulled the trigger, twice.

The way Pamela's body was left on the bathroom floor is so similar to what Dodge County Sheriff's detectives found in Blooming Prairie that a rookie on the beat could have figured it out. It was probably the same gun that killed both Pamela and David, too.

The motive? Pamela is or was Lois' doppelgänger. She has become Lois' new identity.

As detectives are putting the pieces together and coming to that conclusion in the bathroom, Lois is on the run. She abandons her Cadillac Escalade in a park and takes off in Pam's Accura. She's also got Pam's money, credit cards and identification—the ID that Lee County detectives believe prompted Lois to befriend Pamela in the first place.

"[Lois] Riess' mode of operation is to befriend women who resemble her and steal their identities," the Lee County Sheriff's Office says in a statement. The Sheriff's Office also describes her as "armed and dangerous."

Seven

The pursuit of Lois Riess is now a federal case. She's on the run in Pamela's Accura. Everyone knows that. And thanks to Lois' reliance on Pamela's credit cards, it's no secret where she is. But somehow Lois is managing to stay one step ahead of law enforcement.

That doesn't concern police too much. Even when the feds are a step or two behind, investigators—now U.S. Marshals—know where Lois is, or better put, has, been.

Investigators also know Lois is running on Pamela's money. Not only did Lois stop at a Wells Fargo bank on Fort Myers Beach to hit Pam's account for $5,000 before she checked into that hotel in Ocala; she's made three withdrawals of $500 each since then.

Marshals who are hot on her trail do have a concern, however. What happens when Lois maxes out Pam's credit cards? What happens when she runs out of cash? Will Pam find another doppelgänger and put a couple of small-caliber rounds in that mirror image of herself, too?

So this patient cat-and-mouse approach can only go so far. Federal investigators are sure Lois has killed twice. They have no reason to believe she won't do it again. What the marshals don't realize is that killing Pam wasn't easy on Lois. This grandmother from Blooming Prairie stood at the elevator on the fourth floor of Marina Village for nearly fifteen minutes crying and shaking, trying to pull herself together before escaping into the night.

However, marshals do know she's on the road; probably Interstate-10 heading west away from Florida.

But where is Lois, exactly?

Lousiana.

Federal marshals get a hit. They knew eventually they'd get a ping since Lois is using Pam's credit cards. She'd have to stop for gas, if not food. And sure enough, their patience paid off. Lois stops for gas in Louisiana and runs up a $200 tab on one of Pam's cards.

Oh yeah. Old habits die hard. The Marshal's Service gets another hit. Guess what? Lois won a jackpot at a Louisiana casino; Coushatta Casino Resort in Kinder.

Kinder might be a small, dinky, little town at the intersection of highways 165 and 190, about twenty miles north of I-10, Lois' escape route; but it offers the accused double-murderess, who is addicted to gambling's adrenalin rush the respite she needs. A huge, action-packed casino. Lights are flashing, people are gambling, money is changing hands. It's like going to church on Sunday for someone like Lois.

This is no small, out-of-the-way, hole-in-the-wall, gambling house stuck out in the Louisiana bayou known only to locals. No, Coushatta Casino Resort is a top-shelf operation with eleven restaurants and bars, a championship golf course. In its better-than 100,000-square-foot gaming area, there are more slot machines, and gaming tables than Lois could shake one of Pam Hutchinson's C-notes at.

It's also not the kind of place that keeps the secrets of winners and losers. Lois' jackpot win is quickly a matter of public record. And it's no trick for the feds to grab surveillance video of their favorite murder suspect playing the games and driving away in Pam's Accura.

So, now federal investigators know for sure. She's racing Pam's Accura, credit cards, and cash, as fast as humanly possible around the shoreline of the Gulf Coast.

But she's staying ahead of the law. Police are receiving tips that people have seen her car, have seen Lois, but investigators have to admit they've lost her.

"We're working tips, trying to track her down," says Deputy U.S. Marshal John Kinsey. "Hopefully she turns up one way or another."

Two rewards are offered: $1,000 from Florida Crime Stoppers and $5,000 by the US Marshals Service.

Investigators decide to release a press release today with Lois' photo, an explanation of the crimes of which she's accused, and a warning.

From Florida, Lee County Undersheriff Carmine Marceno urges people not to try to capture Lois themselves. This isn't the time for a citizens arrest. After all, Lois has killed twice. And she is considered to be armed and dangerous.

"She is calculated, she's targeted, and she's an absolute cold-blooded killer," Marceno says.

But where's Lois going?

West. Then, maybe south. Could she be going to Mexico?

When she finishes at Coushatta Casino Resort in Kinder and gets back on the road, Lois goes south on Highway 165, back down to U.S. 10.

A quick left and she's on her way to The Lone Star State, Texas.

Where's she going to stop next? Will she meet a new friend? Will federal marshals have a third corpse to add to their investigation?

Those are all open questions that perhaps even Lois would have trouble answering as the small-town woman from Minnesota, suddenly in the U.S Marshal's Service spotlight hits the open road.

Eight

Days go by with no sign of Lois. Ever since she won that Louisiana casino jackpot, the most wanted woman from Minnesota has disappeared from law enforcement's radar.

Federal investigators know Lois is on the road again. That's why they've invested in a rather novel, yet decidedly low-tech method of letting the public see the danger she poses, and at the same time seeking out information from anyone who's crossed Lois' path.

Billboards.

Actually, the campaign isn't all that low-tech. Electronic billboards are flashing a U.S. Marshal's Service Wanted Poster emblazoned with Lois' smiling face to people in cars and trucks as they drive through Texas, New Mexico, Arizona, California, and Nevada.

The billboard messages flashing Lois' face also urge motorists not to try to stop her by themselves. Lois is still considered to be "armed and dangerous." The best advice to anyone who crosses this lady's path; call 911.

Investigators are confident she's heading west after being spotted in Louisiana. But Lois could also be driving south. So Mexican police are being warned to watch out for her, too.

While they might not know precisely where Lois is, marshals are pretty close to her, maybe closer to their prey than they realize.

Lois has been driving Pam's Accura through Texas, clinging close to the Gulf Coast; and she is getting close to Mexico.

She stopped for gas in Corpus Christi, prompting one of the thousands of calls from people who think they've spotted her. This time the callers are correct. And of course, she's still using Pam's credit cards.

From Corpus Christi Lois continues south, heading for the refuge of Mexico. She's so close. Lois is driving along Highway 77 after fueling the Accura in Corpus Christi. It's a straight shot south to the Mexican border which, in Lois' mind, has become her end zone. If she can get into Mexico, the U.S. Marshals, Lois decides, will have that much more trouble finding her.

But first, Lois needs to refuel herself, her/Pam's car again, and maybe make a new friend.

That's just what she does. Lois meets a woman on South Padre Island, twenty-seven miles from the U.S./Mexico border.

She's only about an hour away from at least three border crossing-stations in Brownsville, Texas. Sixty minutes from Mexico. But instead of getting into her car and crossing the border, Lois checks into a Motel 6.

South Padre Island is a fun, swinging, resort town, a favorite of spring breaking college students. So Lois decides that Mexico can wait for a couple of days.

And now she and her new BFF are getting along well enough that Lois is invited to spend a night in the guest bedroom of the woman's house.

This woman, a stranger to Lois, obviously hasn't seen the billboards or any of the cable TV news channels that have made Lois' flight a national story.

If she had, this friendly soul on South Padre Island would never have invited Lois into her house. She would have called 911.

But she didn't. Has Lois found another doppelgänger?

Nine

APRIL 19, 2018

George Higginbotham, the manager of Dirty Al's, a water-front seafood restaurant in South Padre Island, can't stop looking at a woman who is studying a menu before ordering a meal at the bar at about 7pm.

There's really nothing unusual about her. She's smiling like any vacationer would on a beautiful spring evening on South Padre Island. The woman doesn't look nervous. She's not looking back over her shoulder, not twitching, not tapping her fingers. She's totally cool.

But still, George senses something is wrong. He knows this woman from somewhere, but can't put a name with the face. When Lois flips her hair back from her face, it dawns on him.

George is suddenly sure that this is Lois Riess, the woman who police think murdered her husband in Minnesota and a woman in Florida. George remembers Lois flipping her hair the same way on a surveillance video that showed her talking to Pamela Hutchinson at a Fort Meyers bar. Lois is totally calm, cool, and collected but maybe she also senses something is wrong. Lois decides Dirty Al's isn't where she wants to eat. As Lois is leaving the bar, George thinks about tackling her and making a citizen's arrest but remembers the warning that she's armed and dangerous.

Instead, he tells one of his co-workers about his suspicions and calls 911. Another restaurant employee, who's been alerted by George, follows Lois outside as she gets into the Accura and drives off.

Twenty minutes later, five federal deputy marshals following up George's call, find Lois eating dinner in a restaurant not far from Dirty Al's and slap the handcuffs on her. Armed and dangerous? No. George didn't have to worry. Lois is not packing.

Nor does Lois seem surprised to be arrested. It's like she saw it coming. Maybe this is easier than trying to make a new life in Mexico. Chances are Lois wouldn't have been faced with that prospect. There wasn't a guard on either side of the border who didn't have her picture and her wanted poster. Someone would really need to be asleep at the switch to let this woman cross into Mexico.

Ignoring her Miranda rights, Lois is perfectly cooperative and takes the marshals to her Motel 6 room. Investigators discover two pistols — a .22 caliber and a 9-millimeter. They have their murder weapon. It is the .22. Minnesota Bureau of Criminal Apprehension investigators found shell casings where David Riess was gunned down that match the handgun. And, Florida detectives said that was the gun that was used in the slaying of Pam Hutchinson.

One of these guns has to be the murder weapon; the marshals are confident of that. And they also know they've got their woman. If Lois Riess did kill twice; she'll never do it again.

What the marshals don't know is if Lois was planning to kill her new friend in Texas and steal her identity, too. But if that was the plan, she didn't follow through. That woman who invited this accused killer into her house escaped with her life.

Ten

Florida prosecutors say Lois should die for the crimes she's accused of committing. The Sunshine State gets her first, before Minnesota. Lois is as easy-going in her court proceedings as she was when federal marshals arrested her.

She waives a fight over extradition and winds up in the hands of Florida authorities who refuse to give any quarter. A month after a grand jury indicts Lois on a charge of first-degree murder, the State Attorney's Office in Lee County notifies the court that they would see the death penalty against Lois.

Sentencing for a first-degree murder conviction in Florida offers the option of execution or life in prison. The Death Row inmate actually gets to choose. First. prosecutors will have to prove Lois killed Pam in the "cold, calculated, and premeditated manner," required for her execution.

Even though she's been incredibly cooperative, Lois enters a plea of not guilty.

• • • •

UNTIL LOIS' TRIAL IN Florida and then her court case in Minnesota are heard, questions remain.

Assuming Florida and Minnesota law enforcement investigators are correct, how and why did this happen? What motivated this sweet, loving, grandma from Blooming Prairie, Minnesota to murder her husband and then take the life of Pam Hutchinson, her "doppelgänger" in Florida?

Lois' son, Braden, doesn't understand it. He can only imagine that something must have snapped inside of his mom's mind to turn her this evil.

"My whole family is in shock. Nobody ever suspected anything like this. It has devastated our family," Braden told Inside Edition.

Whatever her motivation, Tabitha Lohr Stoops, a cousin of Pam Hutchinson, is confident Lois will have to answer for her sins when she "meets her maker."

Not only does Tabitha hurt from the loss of her cousin, Pam; she's absolutely enraged by what she's seen on the hotel security video of Lois that was recorded in Ocala, Florida after Pam was murdered.

In the video, Lois is seen smiling, laughing, and wearing one of Pam's hats.

At least it looks like one of her cousin's hats to Tabitha.

"When I saw the hat, I just broke down because this was one of Pam's prized possessions," Tabitha says. "This was one of her favorites, and she wore it many times. For me to see this vile woman wearing my cousin's hat after she murdered her was heartbreaking."

Braden says, "It's like a bad movie. I feel like I'm going to wake up and it's going to be back no normal, but it's not."

After admitting that his mom had gambling problems, Braden says, "gambling is a terrible thing that can suck people in, destroy lives." He's not sure how much money Lois lost in one night because of her love of casinos. But he believes she gambled away a $500,000 inheritance.

He also stresses that his mom is a good lady, who was always caring and continually put her kids and her family first, and her concerns second.

Oh no, says Tabitha.

She says Braden needs to understand that Lois should not be thought of as someone's "mother" or "grandmother."

"To me, she surrendered those titles the moment she sunk to a level where she is inhuman. She doesn't deserve those titles anymore. We are a religious family, and I do feel she will meet her maker and be dealt with."

But Braden says his mom shouldn't be judged too harshly, or at the very least, needs to be treated with an understanding of what can happen when a person is addicted to gambling.

"Something happened in her brain that made her snap," Braden says. "She had her own demons."

As of this writing, Braden has not seen his mom since her arrest. But when they do get together, Braden says he'll tell her that he loves her.

Of course, his mother, who has pled not guilty, should be considered innocent until proven guilty.

Bibliography

RICK BUSSLER. "MAN Shot To Death Near BP: Murder investigation prompts manhunt for wife, vehicle." *Times-Independent*, posted 28 March 2018.

Andy Brownell. "Blooming Prairie Woman Accused of Stealing From Murdered Husband." KROC-AM News, posted 28 March 2018.

Jeffrey Jackson. "Murdered man's wife continues to elude authorities." *Owatonna People's Press*, posted 6 April 2018.

Post-Bulletin Staff, "David 'Dave' Riess — Blooming Prairie (Obituary) *Post-Bulletin*, posted 9 April 2018.

John Kinsey, Deputy U.S. Marshall. "U.S. Marshals Lead Manhunt for Female Murder Suspect on a 'Losing Streak.'" U.S. Marshals Service, posted 13 April 2018.

Avi Selk and Lindsey Bever. "Wanted: This gambling grandmother who impersonated a look-alike — then killed her, police say." *Washington Post*, posted 17 April 2018.

Emily Shapiro. "Woman on the run after allegedly killing husband, doppelgänger, in multi-state crime spree." ABC News, posted 17 April 2018.

Tribune Media staff. "Nationwide hunt for 'cold-blooded killer' grandmother after husband, look-alike found dead." Tribune Media, posted 17 April 2018.

KARE Staff. "U.S. Marshals launch Lois Riess billboards." KARE, posted 18 April 2019.

KMSP Staff. "VIDEO: Lois Riess stopped at Iowa gas station the day husband's body was found." KMSP-Fox 9, posted 19 April 2081.

Melissa Montoya and Michael Braun. "Marshal's Service says Lois Ann Riess arrested at restaurant in South Padre Island, Texas." *News-Press*, posted 19 April 2018.

Associated Press staff. "Doppelgänger murder suspect caught in Texas." Associated Press posted 20 April 2018.

CBS Staff. "Fugitive grandma Lois Riess arrested after authorities receive tip in Texas." CBS/AP, posted 20 April 2018.

Michael Braun. "Friends of Lois Riess vacationing tell TV Show about seeing her there," *News-Press*, posted 25 April 2018.

Ariel Zilber. "The moment 'Losing Streak Lois' was arrested by police books after 'fatally shooting her husband and a woman targeted because she looked like her,'" *Daily Mail*/Associated Press, posted 30 April 2018.

KIMT Staff. "Documents detail what woman linked to murders in Florida, Minnesota did before and after alleged killings." posted 1 May 2018, updated 8 February 2019.

Melissa Montoya. "Court docs: Lois Riess was 'distraught, upset' after allegedly killing Pamela Hutchinson." *News-Press*, posted 1 May 2018, updated 2 May 2018.

Katherine Lam. "'Losing Streak Lois' son says his mom 'snapped' before alleged murders."

Fox News, posted 6 May 2018.

Kayla Brantley and Ariel Wilber. "Gambling addict known as 'Losing Streak Lois' pleads NOT guilty to the murders of her husband and a Florida woman whose identity she stole." *Daily Mail*, posted 14 May 2018, updated 15 May 2018.

Justin Doom. "Woman accused of killing husband, doppelgänger, inducted for 1st-degree murder." ABC News, posted 7 June 2018.

Associated Press staff. "Documents Detail Journey of MN Woman Accused of Killing Husband." Associated Press, posted 19 June 2018.

Samuel Chamberlain. "Death penalty sought against 'Losing Streak Lois' Riess in Florida murder." Fox News/Associated Press, posted 3 July 2018.

Andy Brownell. "Minnesota AG Office Now Reviewing Evidence in Lois Riess Case." KROC, posted 20 February 2019.

Mike Bunge. "Gun Found in Lois Riess' Hotel Room Is Linked To Dodge County Killing." KIMT News, posted 20 February 2019, updated 21 February 2019.

Allie Johnson. "Sheriff: Gun found in Lois Riess' hotel room also used in husband's murder." KMSP-Fox 9, posted 21 February 2019.

Other Sources:

Diamond Jo Casino website diamondjoworth.com[1]

Blooming Prairie, Minnesota city-data.com[2]

Weather Underground Weather History: Blooming Prairie, MN/Fort Meyers, FL

Dodge County Sheriff's Office "David Riess Homicide," posted 13 April 2019

---

1.   http://diamondjoworth.com

2.   http://city-data.com

Don't miss out!

Visit the website below and you can sign up to receive emails whenever Rod Kackley publishes a new book. There's no charge and no obligation.

https://books2read.com/r/B-A-BYRB-MOBZ

BOOKS 2 READ

Connecting independent readers to independent writers.

Did you love *Her Own Demons*? Then you should read *Never Forgive, Never Forget* by Rod Kackley!

Venus' mother believes her daughter's husband lured her outside. They fought. He won. Venus' mom wants her daughter back, dead or alive.

Never Forgive, Never Forget: A Shocking True Crime Story by Rod Kackley tells the shocking true crime story of a woman whose fear of her husband seems to turn out to be justified, and the story of a mother's quest to win the return of her child — her best friend — even if it's only to bury her.

The disappearance of Venus Stewart is a shocking true crime story that rocked southwest Michigan and eventually the nation.

The police and her mother were sure Venus' husband killed her. But he was in Newport News, Virginia when the crime was committed in Michigan. The neighbors saw him. He used his credit cards and even paid on his account at his lawyer's office.

And it wasn't just the day that Venus disappeared that her husband was seen in Newport News. He was spotted the next day too. How can anyone be in two places at one time?

Here's something else: no corpse. That's right, the police don't have a body. How can investigators even be sure Venus is dead?

Her mother had to wait more than eight long years — 3,101 days — before finding out what had happened to her child.

A community rose up to stand by Therese McComb and her mission to learn the truth, and after searching for Venus hundreds of times, they stood by Therese at the very end.

Never Forgive, Never Forget: A Shocking True Crime Story is a page-turning, hard-hitting tale of a mother's undying devotion and love for her child; and two police officers' refusal to give up, that you too, will never forget.

Here's another question. If you were the community, the police, the mother; could you ever forgive?

Also by Rod Kackley

A Shocking True Crime Story
True Love, Too Late
Her Best Friend's Killer
She Deserved Better: A Shocking True Crime Story of a
Craigslist Killer
Why Did That Man Kill Uncle George?
Never Forgive, Never Forget
Please Don't Shoot
Kalamazoo's Suitcase Killer
Her Own Demons

A Shocking True Crime Story of Mass Murder
Lustful Desires

Shocking True Crime Stories
Sleeping With The Devil: A Shocking True Crime Story of the
Most Evil Woman in Britain

Who Killed Brittanee Drexel? A Shocking True Crime Story of a Teenager's Murder and a Mother's Grief
Murder! 12 Shocking True Crime Stories

St. Isidore Collection
So Young, So In Love, So Dead: A Serial Killer Thriller
Stories of St. Isidore: From The St. Isidore Collection

Standalone
Sexual Killing: A Shocking True Crime Story
The Devil Made Him Do It: A Shocking True Crime Story of Mass Murder
Mommy Deadliest: A Shocking True Crime Story of a Murdering Mother
Sealed With A Kill: A Shocking True Crime Love Story

About the Author

Rod Kackley is an award-winning author and journalist, with a lifelong fascination of crime, who lives in Grand Rapids, Mich.

Rod also writes crime fiction books in the St. Isidore Collection.

Read more at https://www.rodkackley.com.

Made in the USA
San Bernardino, CA
05 July 2019